D0441202

GOLDEN FRUIT

Nine Lessons about the Fruit of the Spirit

CONCORDIA PUBLISHING HOUSE · SAINT LOUIS

JULIE HALE MASCHHOFF
A Women's Small-Group Bible Study

This Bible study is dedicated to the wonderful women in my small groups. You are each a true blessing in my life. May God continue to bless each of you as we journey through our "golden years."

—Julie Hale Maschhoff

Copyright © 2012 Concordia Publishing House
3558 S. Jefferson Avenue, St. Louis, MO 63118-3968
1-800-325-3040 · www.cph.org

Written by Julie Hale Maschhoff

Art Credits:
Cover art: iStockphoto.com
Background textures: © Shutterstock, Inc.
Pear illustration: © iStockphoto.com
Pear line art illustration: © Gokce Gurellier/Shutterstock, Inc.

Manufactured in the United States of America

1 2 3 4 5 6 7 8 9 10   21 20 19 18 17 16 15 14 13 12

TABLE OF CONTENTS

Suggestions for Small-Group Participants

1. Begin small-group time with prayer.

2. Every participant should feel free to express her thoughts. Comments shared in the small group should remain confidential unless you have received permission to share them outside your group.

3. If your meeting time does not allow you to discuss all of the questions for the week, the leader should choose the questions most meaningful to the group.

4. Close by sharing concerns and prayer requests, then praying together.

As We Begin Our Journey . . .

This Bible study was written with you in mind. Yes, you. If you are a woman (hello, sister!) and a Christian (and even if you are not), I hope you will find God's message in this study, and I look forward to this journey with you. As women in this time of history, we have a big job. We are to be good wives, devoted daughters, loving sisters, supermoms, and cool grandmas. Of course, we must always set the tone for our household—have you heard the saying, "If Mama ain't happy, ain't nobody happy"? If you don't have children, you are to be the fun aunt and the dutiful daughter with lots of time to deal with aging parents. We, as women, are to be emotional, intuitive, creative, hardworking, and supportive of everyone around us. And oh, yes, we should always be healthy and look our best. Are you tired just reading that? I am. I know what a big job we all have. I know we become tired and crabby and just want some time to get away or be alone. I know that as we age, life piles things on: things that sometimes make us sad or scared or downright angry. These burdens weigh us down and threaten to rob our lives of fruitfulness.

However, I also know that God promises us salvation and peace in exchange for our burdens. That is the hard part, isn't it? How can we dare feel free to give Him our burdens, to trust Him with the fruit of our lives, when we are supposed to be in charge of so many things? Well, sister, let's try to figure that out together. As we do, my prayer is that the fruit of the Spirit will bring many blessings to us all.

The Author

> The fruit of the Spirit is love, joy, peace, patience, kindness, goodness, faithfulness, gentleness, self-control; against such things there is no law.
>
> (Galatians 5:22–23)

7

The Vine

> I am the true vine, and My Father
> is the vinedresser.   (John 15:1)

Group Prayer: Father, help us and guide us as we begin this journey of studying the fruit of the Spirit. By Your Spirit, may we all grow in understanding and courage to live out this fruit fully in each stage of our lives. In Jesus' name we pray. Amen.

Acres and acres of grapevines stretch out across gently rolling hills: the beauty of brilliant red, deep purple, or bright green grapes summon up the promise of succulent tastes to come. From popping a ripe, fresh grape into one's mouth to a glass of delicate white wine, grapes provide us with innumerable flavors and tastes. Grapes are the largest fruit crop on earth and are definitely one of God's glorious creations.

Growing grapes is a tedious and very time-consuming endeavor. The grape on the vine is only as good as the vine itself. For delicious grapes, the vine must be treated with a lot of tender loving care. Cindy Newkirk of Steinbeck Vineyard in Paso Robles, California, states that a year of preparation goes into each vine alone. After each growing season, the vines are "put to bed" with heavy irrigation and fertilization.

During the winter months, the vines' branches are pruned to ensure better quality fruit, and in March, the buds swell and shoots begin to sprout. During the growing season, the grapes begin to sweeten as sugar is transported from the leaves to the fruit. The sweet fruit of the vine will not successfully grow if the vine is not meticulously tended by the vine-grower. Let's study the wonderful women of the Bible and see how God produced the fruits of faith in them!

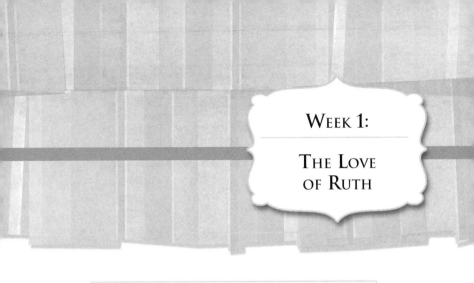

> So now faith, hope, and love abide, these
> three; but the greatest of these is love.
>
> 1 Corinthians 13:13

Group Prayer: Father, help us understand how Christians should love others. Keep us strong as we strive to love those who are difficult to love. Fill us with the love of Christ that we may love others as You have loved us. Amen.

When you hear the word *love*, what comes to mind? Perhaps a favorite song drifts into your consciousness from somewhere in the past. From "Some Enchanted Evening" from the movie *South Pacific* to Elvis's "Love Me Tender," songwriters and singers have expressed their own ideas of love down through history. Poets such as Elizabeth Barrett Browning and Lord Byron have expressed their feelings of love in beautifully written language. That's not to mention the depiction of love in movies, books, and television shows. Our understanding of love is often influenced by our entertainment.

Perhaps the word *love* brings to mind other family members: children, parents, sisters or brothers, and grandchildren, or showing love through the giving of cards and gifts on holidays such as Valentine's Day, Mother's Day, or Father's Day.

Maybe you are an animal lover and love your pet. Do you love chocolate or popcorn or candy bars? We can love almost anything, can't we?

Researchers have identified six types of love:

- *Eros* involves romance and passion.
- *Ludus* is uncommitted love.
- *Storge* refers to a slow-developing, friendship-based love.
- *Pragma* love is a practical, mutually beneficial relationship.
- *Mania* is an obsessive, jealous love.
- *Agape* is a gentle, giving, unconditional type of love.

God speaks to us clearly about how we are to love one another. Depending on the translation, the word *love* is mentioned as many as 508 times in the Bible—more if the word *loved* is counted. Discuss the following verses and identify how the word *love* is used in each verse.

> **Leviticus 19:18:** You shall not take vengeance or bear a grudge against the sons of your own people, but you shall love your neighbor as yourself: I am the LORD.

1. Besides commanding us not to seek revenge or bear a grudge, why did God tell us to love our neighbors?

_____

_____

_____

_____

> **Proverbs 10:12:** Hatred stirs up strife, but love covers all offenses.

2. How can love cover an offense?

_____

_____

_____

_____

1 Peter 4:8: Above all, keep loving one another earnestly, since love covers a multitude of sins.

3. According to this verse, does love make sin go away?

_____

_____

_____

_____

Romans 12:10: Love one another with brotherly affection. Outdo one another in showing honor.

4. How does God expect us to act toward one another?

_____

_____

_____

_____

Ephesians 5:25: Husbands, love your wives, as Christ loved the church and gave Himself up for her.

5. How does God instruct husbands to treat their wives?

_____

_____

_____

John 3:16: For God so loved the world, that He gave His only Son, that whoever believes in Him should not perish but have eternal life.

6. How does it make you feel to realize that God gave His only Son to save us?

_____

_____

_____

_____

The Fruit of Ruth

Then [Naomi] arose with her daughters-in-law to return from the country of Moab, for she had heard in the fields of Moab that the LORD had visited His people and given them food. So she set out from the place where she was with her two daughters-in-law, and they went on the way to return to the land of Judah. But Naomi said to her two daughters-in-law, "Go, return each of you to her mother's house. May the LORD deal kindly with you, as you have dealt with the dead and with me. The LORD grant that you may find rest, each of you in the house of her husband!" Then she kissed them, and they lifted up their voices and wept. And they said to her, "No, we will return with you to your people." But Naomi said, "Turn back, my daughters; why will you go with me? Have I yet sons in my womb that they may become your husbands? Turn back, my daughters; go your way, for I am too old to have a husband. If I should say I have hope, even if I should have a husband this night and should bear sons, would you therefore wait till they were grown? Would you therefore refrain from marrying? No, my daughters, for it is exceedingly bitter to me for your sake that the hand of the LORD has gone out against me." Then they lifted up their voices and wept again. And Orpah kissed her mother-in-law, but Ruth clung to her.

And she said, "See, your sister-in-law has gone back to her people and to her gods; return after your sister-in-law." But Ruth said, "Do not urge me to leave you or to return from following you. For where you go I will go, and where you lodge I will lodge. Your people shall be my people, and your God my God. Where you die I will die, and there will I be buried. May the LORD do so to me and more also if anything but death parts me from you." And when Naomi saw that she was determined to go with her, she said no more.

(Ruth 1:6–18)

7. What is the setting for the Book of Ruth?

_____

_____

_____

_____

8. Naomi was left without her husband and two sons. How does she say she feels (v. 13)?

_____

_____

_____

_____

9. How did Ruth and Orpah exhibit love for their mother-in-law?

_____

_____

_____

_____

10. What did Ruth say when she stayed with Naomi? Is that love?

_____

_____

_____

_____

11. What can we learn from this story?

_____

_____

_____

_____

Let's Talk about Love

_____

_____

_____

_____

12. Discussion starter: In your own words, describe love.

_____

_____

_____

_____

13. Do you remember your first love? Describe it here:

_____

_____

_____

_____

14. How was that love different from love you experienced later in life?

_____

_____

_____

_____

15. How has God helped you love your family throughout your life?

_____

_____

_____

_____

a. Love for parents

_____

_____

_____

b. Love for spouse

_____

_____

c. Love for in-laws

_____

_____

_____

d. Love for children and grandchildren

_____

_____

_____

16. Do you find anyone in particular hard to love? Why?

_____

_____

_____

_____

17. Describe love, as you view it, in this season of your life.

_____

_____

_____

_____

God's Promise

God promises us in His Word that He loves us with an everlasting love. He binds His love to us in our Baptism, and so He will not leave us or forsake us, even when we do not listen to Him or when we turn away from Him. God loves us so much that He gave His only Son to die for us, so that we will live in eternity with Him. Isn't it absolutely incredible that

God could love us so much that He sacrificed His only Son for us? Today, God continues to love us, speaking words of forgiveness in Absolution and assuring us of His continuing love in Holy Communion. Could we ask for more? I don't think so. His love for us is an everlasting love, and that love now dwells within us. His love for us empowers us to love others truly. Ask God to help you do just that.

Challenge of the Week: Identify someone you (or society) feel is unlovable. Reach out to that person in Christian love.

Closing Prayer: Father, we thank You for the love You have shown us by giving Your only Son to die for our sins. We realize we do not love You or others as we should. Forgive us, Lord, according to Your great love, and walk with us each and every day, helping us to grow in love for all. Amen.

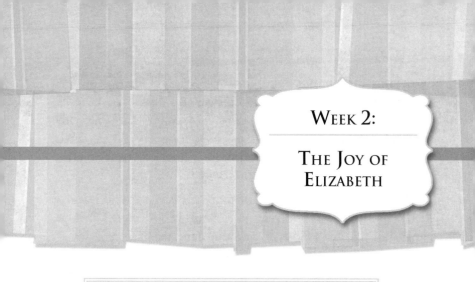

> These things I have spoken to you, that My joy
> may be in you, and that your joy may be full.
>
> John 15:11

Group Prayer: Dear precious Father, help us to see the futility of seeking joy in worldly things. We seek Your joy, and we ask You to fill us with the joy that only You can give. Give us Your joy, which builds others up. Thank You for giving us the joy of a beautiful day and wonderful friends. Amen.

Researchers tell us that contrary to popular belief, the aging population as a whole is not unhappy. There is a mind-body connection to growing older; if, as we age, we are blessed with good health and have planned for financial security, growing older is not so bad. But is there always joy? For those who are growing older plagued by illness and financial problems, the golden years are not so golden. Perhaps you felt joyful watching one of your children graduate from college or get married. Maybe you felt joyful when you saw your grandchild for the first time. These are truly joyful events, but when was the last time you felt uplifted or were filled with the joy of the Lord simply because He is your Lord? Do you remember the refrain from that children's song? "I've got the joy, joy, joy, joy down in my heart. Where? Down in my heart! Where? Down in my heart!" Remember how we sang that song with such gusto when we were kids? How long has it been since you belted out those verses? How long since you really felt the joy of the Lord?

In the Bible, the Greek word for *joy* is *chara*, and it is often translated as "rejoicing" or "gladness." Joy comes from a relationship with God, and no one can take away that joy—not age, not financial circumstances, in fact, no worldly thing. Are you rejoicing and full of gladness about your relationship with God? Let's explore what the Bible tells us about joy, rejoicing, and gladness.

> **Psalm 16:11:** You make known to me the path of life; in Your presence there is fullness of joy; at Your right hand are pleasures forevermore.

1. Where does God tell us we will find joy?

_____

_____

_____

_____

> **Psalm 30:5:** For His anger is but for a moment, and His favor is for a lifetime. Weeping may tarry for the night, but joy comes with the morning.

2. Even if we weep, God promises that what will come in the morning?

_____

_____

_____

_____

Psalm 33:1: Shout for joy in the LORD, O you righteous! Praise befits the upright.

3. What does this verse tell us about rejoicing in the Lord?

_____

_____

_____

_____

Psalm 43:4: Then I will go to the altar of God, to God my exceeding joy, and I will praise You with the lyre, O God, my God.

4. Where does the psalmist go to express his joy in God?

_____

_____

_____

_____

John 16:22: So also you have sorrow now, but I will see you again, and your hearts will rejoice, and no one will take your joy from you.

5. This verse tells us that when we have the joy of the Lord, no one can do what?

_____

_____

_____

_____

James 1:2: Count it all joy, my brothers, when you meet trials of various kinds.

6. Even when we are going through tough times, what are we are to be?

_____

_____

_____

The Fruit of Elizabeth

In the days of Herod, king of Judea, there was a priest named Zechariah, of the division of Abijah. And he had a wife from the daughters of Aaron, and her name was Elizabeth. And they were both righteous before God, walking blamelessly in all the commandments and statutes of the Lord. But they had no child, because Elizabeth was barren, and both were advanced in years. Now while he was serving as priest before God when his division was on duty, according to the custom of the priesthood, he was chosen by lot to enter the temple of the Lord and burn incense. And the whole multitude of the people were praying outside at the hour of incense. And there appeared to him an angel of the Lord standing on the right side of the altar of incense. And Zechariah was troubled when he saw him, and fear fell upon him. But the angel said to him, "Do not be afraid, Zechariah, for your prayer has been heard, and your wife Elizabeth will bear you a son, and you shall call his name John. And you will have joy and gladness, and many will rejoice at his birth, for he will be great before the Lord. And he must not drink wine or strong drink, and he will be filled with the Holy Spirit, even from his mother's womb." . . .

In those days Mary arose and went with haste into the hill country, to a town in Judah, and she entered the house of Zechariah and greeted Elizabeth. And when Elizabeth heard the greeting of Mary, the baby leaped in her womb. And Elizabeth was filled with the Holy Spirit, and she exclaimed with a loud cry, "Blessed are you among women, and blessed is the fruit of your womb! And why is this granted to me that the mother of my Lord should come to me? For behold, when the sound of your greeting came to my ears, the baby in my womb leaped for joy. And blessed is she who believed that there would be a fulfillment of what was spoken to her from the Lord." (Luke 1:5–15, 39–45)

7. What impact did God say that Elizabeth's baby would have?

_____

_____

_____

_____

8. How did Elizabeth experience her joy?

_____

_____

_____

_____

9. Why do you think she was joyful?

_____

_____

_____

10. How did she share her joy with others?

_____

_____

_____

_____

11. As women, what can we learn from this story?

_____

_____

_____

_____

Let's Talk about Joy

12. Discussion starter: In your own words, describe joy:

_____

_____

_____

_____

13. When was the last time you felt truly joyful?

_____

_____

_____

14. How do people look and act when they are joyful?

_____

_____

_____

15. Was the feeling of joy different for you . . .

_____

_____

_____

a. when you were a child?

_____

_____

_____

b. when you were a teenager?

_____

_____

_____

16. How does being joyful feel during this season of your life?

_____

_____

17. Identify ways we can look to Christ to help us maintain joy in this season of life.

_____

_____

_____

_____

God's Promise

God has unending joy for us in Christ. It has been said that peace is joy at rest. That suggests we must have peace before we can have joy. But where do we find peace? In John 14, as Jesus is preparing His disciples for His return to the Father, Jesus promises the Holy Spirit as well as peace. God knew that as fallen humans, we would struggle in our daily lives, so He sent us help to find the peace that only He can provide. This peace, in turn, will help us to be joyful in all circumstances. Through Christ and His promise of peace, you will find God's joy, even in the most dire of circumstances.

> **Challenge of the Week:** When you find yourself in situations that cause you stress or grief, deliberately seek to find joy in that situation. Many people find it helpful to keep a thankfulness journal. Writing down what we are thankful for each and every day can help us be mindful of the blessings in our lives. Perhaps you may want to begin your own thankfulness journal.

Closing Prayer: Dear Lord, we offer our heartfelt thanks for this time spent with sister believers as we learn more about Your Word. We ask that Christ's promise of peace be true for us, so that through Him we may find joy in our own lives and spread Your joy to others. Amen.

> Peace I leave with you; My peace I give to you.
> Not as the world gives peace do I give to you.
> Let not your hearts be troubled, neither let them
> be afraid. (John 14:27)

Group Prayer: Heavenly Father, we come before You today as sinners, full of anxiousness and seeking Your peace. We need to be reminded that You are the giver of peace and will always be there to help us through the rough times in life. Help us to rest assured that You will give us peace in all things. Amen.

People look for peace in many places. The 1960s found many young people flashing peace signs. Hippies in tie-dyed shirts might have had the right idea about wanting peace, but they were certainly looking for peace in all the wrong places. Do you remember the bubble bath commercials in which the woman said to the bathtub full of bubbles, "Take me away!"? She was certainly looking for peace. What about seeking peace in the home? Research has shown that constant bickering at home has a detrimental effect on all living there. Then again, there are those comforting words, "Rest in peace," which are often spoken at a funeral. We are all seeking peace.

As humans, we are simply not able to sustain a peaceful life on our own. However, in the worship service before Communion, the pastor speaks the words called the Pax Domini, saying, "The peace of the Lord be with you always" (*LSB*, p. 163). While we often look for peace in various places, God, with His infinite forgiveness, is the only true way to find peace. Yet Christians, it seems, are as guilty as the general population of seeking peace from places that can offer no peace at all. Why is that? Why do we not trust God to give us peace? Why do we ignore the Word of the Lord when He tells us He is the only true giver of peace? Let's explore Scripture for God's peace, the only true peace there is.

> **Psalm 119:165:** Great peace have those who love Your law; nothing can make them stumble.

1. How does loving God's Law bring peace?

_____

_____

_____

_____

> **Proverb 3:1–2:** My son, do not forget my teaching, but let your heart keep my commandments, for length of days and years of life and peace they will add to you.

2. Why does God instruct us to "let [our] heart keep [His] commandments"?

_____

_____

_____

_____

Isaiah 48:18: Oh that you had paid attention to My commandments! Then your peace would have been like a river, and your righteousness like the waves of the sea.

3. How has God guaranteed we can have "peace . . . like a river"?

_____

_____

_____

_____

John 16:33: I have said these things to you, that in Me you may have peace. In the world you will have tribulation. But take heart; I have overcome the world.

4. In the midst of tribulations, where can we find peace?

_____

_____

_____

_____

Romans 5:1: Therefore, since we have been justified by faith, we have peace with God through our Lord Jesus Christ.

5. What kind of peace does being justified by faith give?

_____

_____

_____

_____

Colossians 3:15: And let the peace of Christ rule in your hearts, to which indeed you were called in one body. And be thankful.

6. Where does Christ's peace rule? Will that help us be thankful?

_____

_____

_____

_____

2 Thessalonians 3:16: Now may the Lord of peace Himself give you peace at all times in every way. The Lord be with you all.

7. How is it possible to have "peace at all times in every way"?

_____

_____

_____

_____

The Fruit of Hannah

[Elkanah] had two wives. The name of the one was Hannah, and the name of the other, Peninnah. And Peninnah had children, but Hannah had no children. Now this man used to go up year by year from his city to worship and to sacrifice to the LORD of hosts at Shiloh, where the two sons of Eli, Hophni and Phinehas, were priests of the LORD. On the day when Elkanah sacrificed, he would give portions to Peninnah his wife and to all her sons and daughters. But to Hannah he gave a double portion, because he loved her, though the LORD had closed her womb. And her rival used to provoke her grievously to irritate her, because the LORD had closed her womb. So it went on year by year. As often as she went up to the house of the LORD, she used to provoke her. Therefore Hannah wept and would not eat. And Elkanah, her husband, said to her, "Hannah, why do you weep? And why do you not eat? And why is your heart sad? Am I not more to you than ten sons?"

After they had eaten and drunk in Shiloh, Hannah rose. Now Eli the priest was sitting on the seat beside the doorpost of the temple of the LORD. She was deeply distressed and prayed to the LORD and wept bitterly. And she vowed a vow and said, "O LORD of hosts, if You will indeed look on the affliction of Your servant and remember me and not forget Your servant, but will give to Your servant a son, then I will give him to the LORD all the days of his life, and no razor shall touch his head."

As she continued praying before the LORD, Eli observed her mouth. Hannah was speaking in her heart; only her lips moved, and her voice was not heard. Therefore Eli took her to be a drunken woman. And Eli said to her, "How long will you go on being drunk? Put away your wine from you." But Hannah answered, "No, my lord, I am a woman troubled in spirit. I have drunk neither wine nor strong drink, but I have been pouring out my soul before the LORD. Do not regard your servant as a worthless woman, for all along I have been speaking out of my great anxiety and vexation." Then Eli answered, "Go in peace, and the God of Israel grant your petition that you have made to Him." And she said, "Let your servant find favor in your eyes." Then the woman went her way and ate, and her face was no longer sad.

They rose early in the morning and worshiped before the LORD; then they went back to their house at Ramah. And Elkanah knew Hannah his wife, and the LORD remembered her. And in due time Hannah conceived and bore a son, and she called his name Samuel, for she said, "I have asked for him from the LORD." (1 Samuel 1:2–20)

8. What is the setting for this story?

_____

_____

_____

_____

9. Why was Hannah so distraught about not having a child?

_____

_____

_____

10. How did Hannah finally find peace? Where did it come from (vv. 17–18)?

_____

_____

_____

_____

11. What is God's message to you in this story?

_____

_____

_____

_____

Let's Talk about Peace

12. Discussion starter: What does peace mean to you?

_____

_____

_____

13. Share a time when you were not at peace.

_____

_____

_____

14. Describe a time when you were at peace.

_____

_____

_____

15. Is it easier to be at peace as a young person or as someone in the later season of life?

_____

_____

16. What does "the peace of God, which surpasses all understanding" (Philippians 4:7), mean to you?

_____

_____

_____

_____

17. List ways that God has promised peace to you.

_____

_____

_____

_____

God's Promise

Our loving Father guarantees our eternal salvation by giving us the gift of His only Son, Jesus Christ. He reassures us of His continual presence in our earthly lives through Holy Communion. Knowing that He has forgiven us and that we will spend eternity in the presence of God, we leave the Communion rail singing, "Lord, now You let Your servant go in peace" (*LSB*, p. 165). As women, we can find in Christ a deep, abiding peace, and in turn we become instruments of God's peace. Just as Hannah did, go to God in prayer and supplication and hear the words of the Lord, "Go in peace" (1 Samuel 1:17). Leave your troubles there with Him. He can handle it for you, and He will. Go in peace!

 Challenge of the Week: Ask God to give you peace in an area of your life that is causing you concern. Attempt to live that peace this week.

Closing Prayer: Dear Father, You have promised us peace in Christ. You have given us instructions on how to live in peace. We ask that the Holy Spirit fill us with the peace that only You can give. Amen.

> Be still before the LORD and wait patiently for
> Him; fret not yourself over the one who
> prospers in his way, over the man who carries
> out evil devices! Refrain from anger, and forsake
> wrath! Fret not yourself; it tends only to evil.
> For the evildoers shall be cut off, but those who
> wait for the LORD shall inherit the land.
>
> (Psalm 37:7–9)

Group Prayer: Our most precious heavenly Father, as women we so often struggle with a lack of patience. We ask that You grant us patience at the times we need it. Help us to understand how Mary was able to be so patient. Amen.

Have you seen the cartoon that says, "God, grant me patience and give it to me *now*"? How rare it is anymore to hear the phrase, "She has the patience of Job"! We are a nation of drive-throughs for dinner, for medications, and for coffee. These conveniences have added to our lack of collective patience.

Our lack of patience is as evident on the highway as it is in the marketplace. We impatiently complain when people don't go fast enough or judge them when they go too fast. We even have a name for it now: road rage. Worse, have you ever been in line for a great sale at your favorite department store? Talk about complete disregard for others and a lack of patience! Sadly, Black Friday has created such a lack of patience in customers that some store employees have been trampled by people wanting the best deals.

Much research has been done on the topic of patience. Some research says patience is a personality trait; other researchers believe it is a skill that can be learned. Research has shown that having patience can improve your mental and physical health, increase your chances of healthy relationships, and extend your life. Research on the lack of patience has shown that it can cause everything from high blood pressure to wrinkles on the face. Wouldn't we be better off if we worked on the skill of patience? Even if we were born with a lack of patience, isn't it possible that God can help us develop this trait?

Let's explore what God says about patience in His Word.

Proverbs 15:18: A hot-tempered man stirs up strife, but he who is slow to anger quiets contention.

1. What is a benefit of being patient?

_____

_____

_____

_____

1 Thessalonians 5:14: And we urge you, brothers, admonish the idle, encourage the fainthearted, help the weak, be patient with them all.

2. Scripture tells us to be patient with everyone. Does that mean criminals, those who try to demean Christians, and others who sin against us?

_____

_____

_____

_____

James 1:19–20: Know this, my beloved brothers: let every person be quick to hear, slow to speak, slow to anger; for the anger of man does not produce the righteousness of God.

3. What instructions does this verse give us about patience?

_____

_____

_____

_____

Romans 8:24–25: For in this hope we were saved. Now hope that is seen is not hope. For who hopes for what he sees? But if we hope for what we do not see, we wait for it with patience.

4. We know we are saved by faith. According to this verse, how should we wait for what faith already hopes in?

_____

_____

_____

_____

Revelation 14:12: Here is a call for the endurance of the saints, those who keep the commandments of God and their faith in Jesus.

5. According to this verse, what are we called to do? How can we endure our own impatience?

_____

_____

_____

_____

Psalm 86:15: But You, O Lord, are a God merciful and gracious, slow to anger and abounding in steadfast love and faithfulness.

6. This verse describes aspects of God's character. How does it describe the facet of patience in God's character?

_____

_____

_____

_____

The Fruit of Mary, Mother of Jesus

In the sixth month the angel Gabriel was sent from God to a city of Galilee named Nazareth, to a virgin betrothed to a man whose name was Joseph, of the house of David. And the virgin's name was Mary. And he came to her and said, "Greetings, O favored one, the Lord is with you!" But she was greatly troubled at the saying, and tried to discern what sort of greeting this might be. And the angel said to her, "Do not be afraid,

Mary, for you have found favor with God. And behold, you will conceive in your womb and bear a son, and you shall call His name Jesus. He will be great and will be called the Son of the Most High. And the Lord God will give to Him the throne of His father David, and He will reign over the house of Jacob forever, and of His kingdom there will be no end."

And Mary said to the angel, "How will this be, since I am a virgin?"

And the angel answered her, "The Holy Spirit will come upon you, and the power of the Most High will overshadow you; therefore the child to be born will be called holy—the Son of God." . . .

In those days a decree went out from Caesar Augustus that all the world should be registered. This was the first registration when Quirinius was governor of Syria. And all went to be registered, each to his own town. And Joseph also went up from Galilee, from the town of Nazareth, to Judea, to the city of David, which is called Bethlehem, because he was of the house and lineage of David, to be registered with Mary, his betrothed, who was with child. And while they were there, the time came for her to give birth. And she gave birth to her firstborn son and wrapped Him in swaddling cloths and laid Him in a manger, because there was no place for them in the inn. . . .

Now His parents went to Jerusalem every year at the Feast of the Passover. And when He was twelve years old, they went up according to custom. And when the feast was ended, as they were returning, the boy Jesus stayed behind in

Jerusalem. His parents did not know it, but supposing Him to be in the group they went a day's journey, but then they began to search for Him among their relatives and acquaintances, and when they did not find Him, they returned to Jerusalem, searching for Him. After three days they found Him in the temple, sitting among the teachers, listening to them and asking them questions. And all who heard Him were amazed at His understanding and His answers. And when His parents saw Him, they were astonished. And His mother said to Him, "Son, why have You treated us so? Behold, Your father and I have been searching for You in great distress." And He said to them, "Why were you looking for Me? Did you not know that I must be in My Father's house?" (Luke 1:26–35; 2:1–7, 41–49)

On the third day there was a wedding at Cana in Galilee, and the mother of Jesus was there. Jesus also was invited to the wedding with His disciples. When the wine ran out, the mother of Jesus said to Him, "They have no wine." And Jesus said to her, "Woman, what does this have to do with Me? My hour has not yet come." His mother said to the servants, "Do whatever He tells you." (John 2:1–5)

7. Describe how Mary must have felt when Gabriel appeared to her. Does she seem patient?

_____

_____

_____

_____

8. How must have Mary felt while riding the donkey to Bethlehem? Do you suppose she was patient?

_____

_____

_____

_____

9. What was Mary's reaction when she thought Jesus was lost after the Feast of the Passover?

_____

_____

_____

_____

10. What was Mary's reaction to Jesus at the wedding in Cana? Had Mary learned patience by this point? What was the difference?

_____

_____

_____

_____

11. What can we learn from Mary?

_____

_____

_____

_____

Let's Talk about Patience

12. Discussion starter: What does patience mean to you?

_____

_____

_____

_____

13. Were you more patient when you were younger than you are now?

_____

_____

_____

_____

14. What caused you to lose your patience when you were young?

_____

_____

_____

_____

15. What causes you to lose your patience now, in this season of your life?

_____

_____

_____

_____

16. What would you say to young people today about patience?

_____

_____

_____

_____

17. Has God been part of your journey in seeking patience?

_____

_____

_____

_____

God's Promise

At our Baptism, not only did God make us His holy children, but He also began His patient work of making our lives reflect that holiness. As sinful human beings, we have repeatedly let Him down and given Him every reason to lose patience with us. God has certainly been patient with us, hasn't He? Do we have the ability to be patient? While in many circumstances it is certainly hard to be patient, we should always strive to be patient with others. God, who is patient with us, patiently works to produce His patience in us. Let's pray that His work is completed in us.

> **Challenge of the Week:** Face the person with whom you have no patience and put him or her in the hands of God. Ask God to give you patience that is evident to that person.

Closing Prayer: Father God, we ask that You grant us the ability to be patient with those things we hold in our hearts. We realize that only You can grant us the patience we need. Walk with us each day this week as we work on being patient. Amen.

52

Week 5:

The Kindness of Abigail

> Be kind to one another, tenderhearted, forgiving one another, as God in Christ forgave you.
>
> (Ephesians 4:32)

Group Prayer: Our heavenly Father, it is our desire to live in kindness as You would have us live. You have been so kind to us, and we truly want to be kind to others. Send Your Holy Spirit to each of us, so that we may live each day treating others with kindness. Amen.

What does it mean to be kind? A relatively new phrase is "random acts of kindness," coined to help us remember that we are to be kind to one another. While that is not necessarily a religious phrase, many people do seem to be trying to be kinder to one another. Does kindness translate into an act, that is, something you do for another? Or is kindness something deeper, something that stems from the heart? Can a person do a kind thing but not be a kind person? Do kind people sometimes commit unkind acts?

In response to all the bullying that is occurring in schools, the value of kindness is being taught in classrooms across the country. Can a bully be taught to act kindly toward a fellow classmate? These are hard questions to answer, but the text from Ephesians gives us straightforward instructions. We are to be kind to others, forgiving them their faults just as God was so kind to us that He gave His Son, Jesus Christ, to forgive us. That is certainly more than a "random act of kindness," isn't it?

Roman philosopher Seneca said "wherever there is a human being, there is an opportunity for kindness." From our own experience, we know that we respond better when kindness is shown to us. Therefore, we should, in turn, treat everyone (and everything) with kindness. True kindness doesn't pick and choose, does not want anything in return, and is given freely. Only God, our heavenly Father, can help us grow in true kindness toward others.

Let's see what the Bible says about kindness.

> **1 Corinthians 13:4–5a:** Love is patient and kind; love does not envy or boast; it is not arrogant or rude.

1. Describe love according to this verse.

_____

_____

_____

_____

> **Proverbs 11:17:** A man who is kind benefits himself, but a cruel man hurts himself.

2. What does this verse tell us that God (and others) desire from us?

_____

_____

_____

Ephesians 4:32: Be kind to one another, tender-hearted, forgiving one another, as God in Christ forgave you.

3. How are we to treat our fellow man?

_____

_____

_____

_____

Colossians 3:12: Put on then, as God's chosen ones, holy and beloved, compassionate hearts, kindness, humility, meekness, and patience.

4. Who is to put on "compassionate hearts, kindness, humility, meekness, and patience"?

_____

_____

_____

_____

Luke 6:35: But love your enemies, and do good, and lend, expecting nothing in return, and your reward will be great, and you will be sons of the Most High, for He is kind to the ungrateful and the evil.

5. What do we learn from this verse about the nature of God?

_____

_____

_____

_____

Isaiah 54:10: "For the mountains may depart and the hills be removed, but My steadfast love shall not depart from you, and My covenant of peace shall not be removed," says the LORD, who has compassion on you.

6. According to this verse, for what can we depend on the Lord?

The Fruit of Abigail

And there was a man in Maon whose business was in Carmel. The man was very rich; he had three thousand sheep and a thousand goats. He was shearing his sheep in Carmel. Now the name of the man was Nabal, and the name of his wife Abigail. The woman was discerning and beautiful, but the man was harsh and badly behaved; he was a Calebite. David heard in the wilderness that Nabal was shearing his sheep. So David sent ten young men. And David said to the young men, "Go up to Carmel, and go to Nabal and greet him in my name. And thus you shall greet him: 'Peace be to you, and peace be to your house, and peace be to all that you have. I hear that you have shearers. Now your shepherds have been with us, and we did them no harm, and they missed nothing all the time they were in Carmel. Ask your young men, and they will tell you. Therefore let my young men find favor in your eyes, for we come on a feast day. Please give whatever you have at hand to your servants and to your son David.' "

When David's young men came, they said all this to Nabal in the name of David, and then they waited. And Nabal answered David's servants, "Who is David? Who is the son of Jesse? There are many servants these days who are breaking away from their masters. Shall I take my bread and my water and my meat that I have killed for my shearers and give it to men who come from I do not know where?" So David's young men turned away and came back and told him all this. And David said to his men, "Every man strap on his sword!" And every man of them strapped on his sword. David also strapped on his sword. And about four hundred men went up after David, while two hundred remained with the baggage.

But one of the young men told Abigail, Nabal's wife, "Behold, David sent messengers out of the wilderness to greet our master, and he railed at them. Yet the men were very good to us, and we suffered no harm, and we did not miss anything when we were in the fields, as long as we went with them. They were a wall to us both by night and by day, all the while we were with them keeping the sheep. Now therefore know this and consider what you should do, for harm is determined against our master and against all his house, and he is such a worthless man that one cannot speak to him." Then Abigail made haste and took two hundred loaves and two skins of wine and five sheep already prepared and five seahs of parched grain and a hundred clusters of raisins and two hundred cakes of figs, and laid them on donkeys. (1 Samuel 25:2–18)

7. What type of man was Abigail's husband, Nabal?

_____

_____

_____

_____

8. In spite of this, how does the Bible describe Abigail?

_____

_____

_____

_____

9. Why do you suppose one of David's men approached Abigail?

_____

_____

_____

_____

10. How does her reaction to the plight of David's men demonstrate kindness?

_____

_____

_____

11. What can we learn from Abigail?

_____

_____

_____

_____

Let's Talk about Kindness

12. Discussion starter: What does it mean to be kindhearted?

_____

_____

_____

_____

13. Were you taught as a child to be kind?

_____

_____

_____

_____

14. Do you find it easier to be kind to others as you grow older?

_____

_____

_____

_____

15. Discuss acts of kindness that you have witnessed or experienced.

_____

_____

_____

_____

16. Do you think people can be kind if they are not Christian?

_____

_____

_____

_____

17. To what type of person is it not easy to be kind?

_____

_____

_____

_____

God's Promise

God has shown each and every one of us great kindness in many ways. The Scriptures tell us that in kindness He gives rain in its season and crops for our food (Leviticus 26:4). He kindly gives us the joy of family and friends. However, even if we didn't have these things, we would still know of God's kindness toward us simply by looking at Jesus Christ and our Baptism into Him. Titus 3:4–6 reminds us, "But when the goodness and loving kindness of God our Savior appeared,

He saved us, not because of works done by us in righteousness, but according to His own mercy, by the washing of regeneration and renewal of the Holy Spirit, whom He poured out on us richly through Jesus Christ our Savior." The most important gift of kindness that God has given is His only Son, Jesus Christ, through whom we have eternal life. His Son, Jesus, shows us exactly what kindness is. Ask God for a heart filled with His kindness, which will lead to kind actions toward others.

> **Challenge of the Week:** Strive to be kind from the heart, and share that kindness with others.

Closing Prayer: Our heavenly Father, we ask that You go with us every step of the way this week and help us to be kind to others. Grant us opportunities to be kind to others, as You have been kind to us. In Jesus' name we pray. Amen.

WEEK 6:

THE GOODNESS OF DORCAS (TABITHA)

> And you shall do what is right and good in the sight of the LORD, that it may go well with you, and that you may go in and take possession of the good land that the LORD swore to give to your fathers. (Deuteronomy 6:18)

Group Prayer: Dear Father, as we strive to live for You, please help us to show Your goodness to those around us. Fill our hearts with the desire to be good, even as Your Son, Jesus, is good. We thank You for all the goodness You have shown us in Him. Amen.

How many times did you sing the well-known song as a child and wonder whether Santa would pass right by your house because you hadn't been good enough, because you cried or pouted? How many times did your parents say, "You better be good, because Santa is watching, and when he comes your name will not be on the 'good' list"? Regardless of our age, our culture still rewards good behavior with gifts, treats, and privileges.

In our vocabulary today, the word *good* is used in many different contexts. Aside from behavior being good or bad, we wonder if the meat is still good; we might feel good; someone or something may smell good; hopefully, the brakes on your car are good. We often tell children to eat their veggies because "They are good for you!" People have good eyesight. We might compliment someone by saying, "That looks really good on you." In a biblical sense, the word *good* always refers to something beneficial from God. The word *goodness* is used forty-eight times in the King James Version. It is evident that God is trying to tell us something about goodness. God is the ultimate good, and what He does for us is always good.

Let's explore how the word *good* is used in Scripture.

> **Psalm 31:19:** Oh, how abundant is Your goodness, which You have stored up for those who fear You and worked for those who take refuge in You, in the sight of the children of mankind!

1. According to this verse, in what is God abounding?

_____

_____

_____

_____

> **Amos 5:14:** Seek good, and not evil, that you may live; and so the LORD, the God of hosts, will be with you, as you have said.

2. What does this verse tell us will be the result of seeking good?

_____

_____

_____

_____

> **Mark 10:18:** Jesus said to him, "Why do you call

Me good? No one is good except God alone."

3. What is Jesus saying to the person to whom He is speaking?

_____

_____

_____

_____

Isaiah 1:17: Learn to do good; seek justice, correct oppression; bring justice to the fatherless, plead the widow's cause.

4. This verse tells us that we can learn to do what?

_____

_____

_____

_____

Ephesians 2:10: For we are His workmanship, created in Christ Jesus for good works, which God prepared beforehand, that we should walk in them.

5. This verse shows that we were created for what purpose?

_____

_____

_____

_____

The Fruit of Dorcas (Tabitha)

Now there was in Joppa a disciple named Tabitha, which, translated, means Dorcas. She was full of good works and acts of charity. In those days she became ill and died, and when they had washed her, they laid her in an upper room. Since Lydda was near Joppa, the disciples, hearing that Peter was there, sent two men to him, urging him, "Please come to us without delay." So Peter rose and went with them. And when he arrived, they took him to the upper room. All the widows stood beside him weeping and showing tunics and other garments that Dorcas made while she was with them. But Peter put them all outside, and knelt down and prayed; and turning to the body he said, "Tabitha, arise." And she opened her eyes, and when she saw Peter she sat up. And he gave her his hand and raised her up. Then calling the saints and widows, he presented her alive. And it became known throughout all Joppa, and many believed in the Lord. (Acts 9:36–42)

6. This is the only time Dorcas is mentioned in the Bible. What are the first words used to describe her?

_____

_____

_____

_____

7. For what was Dorcas known?

_____

_____

_____

_____

8. Why did Peter travel from Joppa to Lydda to come to Dorcas's deathbed?

_____

_____

_____

_____

9. By whose power did Peter bring Dorcas back to life?

_____

_____

_____

_____

10. Ultimately, Dorcas's good deeds and Peter's miracles brought glory to whom?

_____

_____

_____

_____

Let's Talk about Goodness

11. Discussion starter: What is the first thing that comes to mind when you hear the word *good*?

_____

_____

_____

12. When you were a child, were you led to believe you were good?

13. List some ways you use the word *good*.

14. Are all people who do good things believers in the Lord?

15. Do you believe you are a good person?

16. Discuss how God has been good to you.

God's Promise

God is so good, isn't He? He has been good to us in so many ways. We know from reading Scripture that God wants us to do good and to be good. We can also rest assured that Jesus Christ died for us even though we are not perfectly good. In our Baptism, He washes away all the sin that separates us from God. God's goodness has saved us, and God's goodness works through us to bring good to others. God is good!

Challenge of the Week: Dear Father, help us this week to see Your goodness in those around us. Help us to be good because we love You.

Closing Prayer: Thank You, Father, for allowing us to live in Your goodness. Help us this week to show goodness to others, so that we may glorify Your name. Amen.

> Know therefore that the LORD your God is God, the faithful God who keeps covenant and steadfast love with those who love Him and keep His commandments, to a thousand generations.
>
> (Deuteronomy 7:9)

Group Prayer: Our most gracious heavenly Father, we give You all praise and glory for the blessings You have granted to each and every one of us. We ask for Your help in growing in faithfulness to You. You have been ever faithful to us, and we thank You for that. In Your Son's most holy name we pray. Amen.

When Jimmy Carter asked Mother Theresa how she could possibly save all those people in the slums of India, she replied, "God didn't call me to be successful; He called me to be faithful." What a wise woman she was. She understood that the task in front of her was daunting, but if she quit, none would be saved. Mother Theresa had the understanding that we should all seek. She knew how to be faithful. Being faithful is a virtue that most people find honorable. We are typically faithful to things we are committed to or things we place value on. We often speak of our faithful pets, faithful friends, or faithful employees. Some people are very faithful to their favorite sports teams. People can be faithful supporters of certain charities or elected officials. If we are faithful, others can depend on us. We are assured in Scripture that we can depend on God, because He has been faithful to us throughout history. He has made promises to us, and He has faithfully kept those promises. He wants us to be faithful to Him in all things. With His help, we can be.

Let's explore the faithfulness of God.

> **Deuteronomy 32:4:** The Rock, His work is perfect, for all His ways are justice. A God of faithfulness and without iniquity, just and upright is He.

1. Of which characteristic of God does this verse assure us?

_____

_____

_____

_____

> **Psalm 36:5:** Your steadfast love, O LORD, extends to the heavens, Your faithfulness to the clouds.

2. Describe God's faithfulness:

_____

_____

_____

> **1 Corinthians 10:13:** No temptation has overtaken you that is not common to man. God is faithful, and He will not let you be tempted beyond your ability, but with the temptation He will also provide the way of escape, that you may be able to endure it.

3. Because God is faithful, of what can we be confident that He will do?

_____

_____

_____

_____

1 John 1:9: If we confess our sins, He is faithful and just to forgive us our sins and to cleanse us from all unrighteousness.

4. This verse tells us that if we confess our sins, what is God faithful to do?

_____

_____

_____

_____

Lamentations 3:22–24: The steadfast love of the LORD never ceases; His mercies never come to an end; they are new every morning; great is Your faithfulness. "The LORD is my portion," says my soul, "therefore I will hope in Him."

5. What are the results of God's love for us?

_____

_____

_____

_____

Revelation 2:10: Do not fear what you are about to suffer. Behold, the devil is about to throw some of you into prison, that you may be tested, and for ten days you will have tribulation. Be faithful unto death, and I will give you the crown of life.

6. Is faithfulness possible even during hardship?

_____

_____

_____

_____

The Fruit of Deborah

Now Deborah, a prophetess, the wife of Lappidoth, was judging Israel at that time. She used to sit under the palm of Deborah between Ramah and Bethel in the hill country of Ephraim, and the people of Israel came up to her for judgment. She sent and summoned Barak the son of Abinoam from Kedesh-naphtali and said to him, "Has not the LORD, the God of Israel, commanded you, 'Go, gather your men at Mount Tabor, taking 10,000 from the people of Naphtali and the people of Zebulun. And I will draw out Sisera, the general of Jabin's army, to meet you by the river Kishon with his chariots and his troops, and I will give him into your hand'?" Barak said to her, "If you will go with me, I will go, but if you will not go with me, I will not go." And she said, "I will surely go with you. Nevertheless, the road on which you are going will not lead to your glory, for the Lord will sell Sisera into the hand of a woman." Then Deborah arose and went with Barak to Kedesh. And Barak called out Zebulun and Naphtali to Kedesh. And 10,000 men went up at his heels, and Deborah went up with him.

Now Heber the Kenite had separated from the Kenites, the descendants of Hobab the father-in-law of Moses, and had pitched his tent as far away as the oak in Zaanannim, which is near Kedesh. When Sisera was told that Barak the son of Abinoam had gone up to Mount Tabor, Sisera called out all his chariots, 900 chariots of iron, and all the men who were with him, from Harosheth-hagoyim to the river Kishon. And Deborah said to Barak, "Up! For this is the day in which the Lord has given Sisera into your hand. Does not the Lord go out before you?" So Barak went down from Mount Tabor with 10,000 men following him. And the Lord routed Sisera and all his chariots and all his army before Barak by the edge of the sword. And Sisera got down from his chariot and fled away on foot. And Barak pursued the chariots and the army to Harosheth-hagoyim, and all the army of Sisera fell by the edge of the sword; not a man was left. (Judges 4:4–16)

7. Why was it unusual for Deborah to be a judge at this time in history?

_____

_____

_____

_____

8. Besides being a judge, what else was Deborah?

_____

_____

_____

_____

9. How was Deborah faithful in both of these roles?

_____

_____

_____

_____

10. Who benefited from Deborah's faithfulness? How?

_____

_____

_____

_____

11. What is God telling us in this story?

_____

_____

_____

_____

Let's Talk about Faithfulness

12. Discussion starter: In what ways do we use the word *faithful*?

_____

_____

_____

_____

13. How important is faithfulness to you?

_____

_____

_____

_____

14. What other words describe faithfulness?

_____

_____

_____

_____

15. How has God shown His faithfulness to you?

_____

_____

_____

_____

16. How have you shown your faithfulness to God?

_____

_____

_____

_____

17. How can you grow in faithfulness to God?

_____

_____

_____

_____

God's Promise

In Scripture, God shows over and over that He is a faithful God. He tells each of us that He will not forsake or forget us. What peace that promise should give us! We can trust in God's faithfulness because He sent His only Son to die on the cross for our sins, just as He promised. We know God promises in in His Word that the Holy Spirit strengthens us to help us remain faithful. What a wonderful promise that is. We can then face the world knowing that God walks with us each step of the way. How faithful is our God!

Challenge of the Week: Strive to grow in your faithfulness to God. Remind yourself daily that He has been faithful to you.

Closing Prayer: Dear God, help us to grow in faithfulness to You. Even when we are faced with daunting tasks or frightening situations, help us to be faithful to Your Word. Amen.

PERSONAL
JOURNAL

> A soft answer turns away wrath,
> but a harsh word stirs up anger.
>
> (Proverbs 15:1)

Group Prayer: Dear Father, we ask that You fill us with Your Holy Spirit as we study Your Word. Help us to grow in gentleness so that we may treat others gently, just as You have treated us. Thank You for the stories that help us learn about how to be gentle. In Jesus' name we pray. Amen.

What do you think of when you hear the word *gentle*? Something tender or soft or fragile? When a new baby arrives in a family, the older children are often reminded to be gentle so they don't hurt the baby in some way. We might remind small children to be gentle with Grandma's fine china, so we won't have it in a thousand pieces all over the floor!

When we treat people with gentleness, they are typically valuable to us. When we treat objects with gentleness, the object is typically fragile. Looking at the word *gentle* from the opposite point of view might be helpful. The words *rough*, *careless*, or *crude* might come to mind. While gentleness is like a delicate whisper, the opposite leaves one battered by gale-force winds. Often, these winds leave people scarred for life. Gentleness builds up; roughness tears down.

Remember the star of the old television series *Gentle Ben*? This huge, fierce-looking grizzly bear was incredibly gentle, at least in the fantasy land of television. That contrast illustrates how humans oftentimes act. Our sinful natures cause us to behave with the instinctive nature of the grizzly bear. However, through the grace of God, we can learn to be gentle. Difficult? Absolutely! Possible? With God's help, absolutely!

Let's explore what God says about gentleness.

Philippians 4:5: Let your reasonableness be known to everyone. The Lord is at hand.

1. The word *reasonableness* is sometimes translated *gentleness*. To whom should we show gentleness, and why?

_____

_____

_____

1 Timothy 6:11: But as for you, O man of God, flee these things. Pursue righteousness, godliness, faith, love, steadfastness, gentleness.

2. What does this verse tell us to pursue?

_____

_____

_____

Matthew 11:29: Take My yoke upon you, and learn from Me, for I am gentle and lowly in heart, and you will find rest for your souls.

3. What does this verse tell us about the nature of God?

_____

_____

_____

_____

> **2 Corinthians 10:1:** I, Paul, myself entreat you, by the meekness and gentleness of Christ—I who am humble when face to face with you, but bold toward you when I am away!

4. From where does Paul say his gentleness comes?

_____

_____

_____

_____

> **Ephesians 4:1–2:** I therefore, a prisoner for the Lord, urge you to walk in a manner worthy of the calling to which you have been called, with all humility and gentleness, with patience, bearing with one another in love.

5. Because we are called by God, with what are we to treat others?

_____

_____

_____

_____

The Fruit of Mary, Sister of Martha

Now as they went on their way, Jesus entered a village. And a woman named Martha welcomed Him into her house. And she had a sister called Mary, who sat at the Lord's feet and listened to His teaching. But Martha was distracted with much serving. And she went up to Him and said, "Lord, do You not care that my sister has left me to serve alone? Tell her then to help me." But the Lord answered her, "Martha, Martha, you are anxious and troubled about many things, but one thing is necessary. Mary has chosen the good portion, which will not be taken away from her." (Luke 10:38–42)

Six days before the Passover, Jesus therefore came to Bethany, where Lazarus was, whom Jesus had raised from the dead. So they gave a dinner for Him there. Martha served, and Lazarus was one of those reclining with Him at table. Mary therefore took a pound of expensive ointment made from pure nard, and anointed the feet of Jesus and wiped His feet with her hair. The house was filled with the fragrance of the perfume. But Judas Iscariot, one of His disciples (he who was about to betray Him), said, "Why was this ointment not sold for three hundred denarii and given to the poor?" He said this, not because he cared about the poor, but because he was a thief, and having charge of the moneybag he used to help himself to what was put into it. Jesus said, "Leave her alone, so that she may keep it for the day of My burial. The poor you always have with you, but you do not always have Me." (John 12:1–8)

6. Describe the settings for these two stories.

7. What do both of these stories reveal about Mary?

8. In what ways did the two sisters differ in their preparations for spending time with Jesus?

9. How did Mary treat Jesus with gentleness?

10. Did Jesus treat Mary with gentleness?

Let's Talk about Gentleness

11. Discussion starter: What does the word *gentle* mean to you?

_____

_____

_____

_____

12. How does society view gentleness today?

_____

_____

_____

_____

13. How can we exhibit gentleness in our lives?

_____

_____

_____

_____

14. What can you do to develop an attitude of gentleness?

_____

_____

_____

_____

15. Is there something that prevents you from being gentle?

_____

_____

16. What issue in your life would benefit from more gentleness?

God's Promise

In the gentle waters of our Baptism, our heavenly Father has washed away our sins and adopted us as His children. He promises to answer our prayers. If we ask and trust Him to help us be gentle to others, we will be. When we are angry or stressed, if we turn to God, He will let His blessing of gentleness rain down upon us. Then we can be as gentle with others as Jesus was. Rest assured that His gentleness toward you will help you treat others with gentleness.

Challenge of the Week: Ponder ways you can treat others with gentleness, and strive to accomplish that this week.

Closing Prayer: Thank You, God, for walking with us through this Bible study. Help us to trust You to fill us with the gentleness that can only come from You. You have treated us with such gentleness; help us to share that with others. Amen.

> Therefore, preparing your minds for action, and being sober-minded, set your hope fully on the grace that will be brought to you at the revelation of Jesus Christ. (1 Peter 1:13)

Group Prayer: Heavenly Father, we ask Your special blessing on each of us as we seek to practice self-control. Help us to be strong when we are weak. Amen.

I don't know about you, but I have a big problem with self-control in some areas. These areas include chocolate, coffee from great little coffee shops, and buying things for my wonderful grandchildren. It seems to me that at this age, I should be able to give in to the things I want. Sounds pretty selfish, doesn't it? I mean, eating lots of chocolate and drinking lots of coffee is really not healthy for my body. And, if I am honest, buying lots of stuff for my grandchildren might not be the best thing for them. Maybe you have a problem with self-control in similar areas. I know some people struggle with gossiping or drinking too much alcohol or using language that isn't pleasing to our Lord. Don't we all struggle with self-control in some ways? What we need—what I need—is strength, which only God can give me as I struggle to control the things that are not helpful or perhaps even downright harmful.

In today's world, we often feel we have earned the right to do anything we want. We don't often filter our language, our behavior, or our thoughts because, well, everyone is doing it, so it must be okay. Right? Wrong! We must learn to practice self-control. Self-control is a biblical teaching and is really a commandment from our Lord. Only He can help us with it. Ask your Lord to give you strength in areas in which you are weak. He promises to help us when we ask. Ask Him for self-control.

Let's explore what the Bible says about self-control.

> **Proverbs 25:28:** A man without self-control is like a city broken into and left without walls.

1. If we have no control over ourselves, what are we like?

_____

_____

_____

_____

> **Titus 1:7–8:** [For an overseer, as God's steward must be above reproach. He must not be arrogant or quick-tempered . . . but hospitable, a lover of good, self-controlled, upright, holy, and disciplined.

2. In this verse, Paul is speaking about those who preach. However, these characteristics can also be said to be required of whom?

_____

_____

_____

2 Peter 1:5–7: For this very reason, make every effort to supplement your faith with virtue, and virtue with knowledge, and knowledge with self-control, and self-control with steadfastness, and steadfastness with godliness, and godliness with brotherly affection, and brotherly affection with love.

3. List the things that the Lord tells us we should strive for as Christians:

_____

_____

_____

_____

Romans 12:1–2: I appeal to you therefore, brothers, by the mercies of God, to present your bodies as a living sacrifice, holy and acceptable to God, which is your spiritual worship. Do not be conformed to this world, but be transformed by the renewal of your mind, that by testing you may discern what is the will of God, what is good and acceptable and perfect.

4. How is Christian transformation accomplished? Who does that work in us?

_____

_____

_____

_____

The Fruit of Esther

Mordecai told him all that had happened to him, and the exact sum of money that Haman had promised to pay into the king's treasuries for the destruction of the Jews. Mordecai also gave him a copy of the written decree issued in Susa for their destruction, that he might show it to Esther and explain it to her and command her to go to the king to beg his favor and plead with him on behalf of her people. And Hathach went and told Esther what Mordecai had said. Then Esther spoke to Hathach and commanded him to go to Mordecai and say, "All the king's servants and the people of the king's provinces know that if any man or woman goes to the king inside the inner court without being called, there is but one law—to be put to death, except the one to whom the king holds out the golden scepter so that he may live. But as for me, I have not been called to come in to the king these thirty days." And they told Mordecai what Esther had said. Then Mordecai told them to reply to Esther, "Do not think to yourself that in the king's palace you will escape any more than all the other Jews. For if you keep silent at this time, relief and deliverance will rise for the Jews from another place, but you and your father's house will perish. And who knows whether you have not come to the kingdom for such a time as this?" Then Esther told them to reply to Mordecai, "Go, gather all the Jews to be found in Susa, and hold a fast on my behalf, and do not eat or drink for three days, night or day. I and my young women will also fast as you do. Then I will go to the king, though it is against the law, and if I perish, I perish." . . .

On the third day Esther put on her royal robes and stood in the inner court of the king's palace, in front of the king's quarters, while the king was sitting on his royal throne inside the throne room opposite the entrance to the palace. And when the king saw Queen Esther standing in the court, she won favor in his sight, and he held out to Esther the golden scepter that was in his hand. Then Esther approached and touched the tip of the scepter. And the king said to her, "What is it, Queen Esther? What is your request? It shall be given you, even to the half of my kingdom." And Esther said, "If it please the king, let the king and Haman come today to a feast that I have prepared for the king." Then the king said, "Bring Haman quickly, so that we may do as Esther has asked." So the king and Haman came to the feast that Esther had prepared. And as they were drinking wine after the feast, the king said to Esther, "What is your wish? It shall be granted you. And what is your request? Even to the half of my kingdom, it shall be fulfilled." Then Esther answered, "My wish and my request is: If I have found favor in the sight of the king, and if it please the king to grant my wish and fulfill my request, let the king and Haman come to the feast that I will prepare for them, and tomorrow I will do as the king has said." (Esther 4:7–16; 5:1–8)

5. What is the setting for this story?

_____

_____

_____

_____

6. How did Esther practice self-control?

7. What did Esther gain by practicing self-control?

8. Discuss what might have happened if Esther had acted hastily.

9. God is not spoken of in the Book of Esther. Does that mean He was not present? How did God help Esther develop self-control?

Let's Talk about Self-Control

10. Discussion starter: In what areas do you struggle with self-control?

_____

_____

_____

_____

11. Are there areas in which you feel you have mastered self-control?

_____

_____

_____

_____

12. How have you been able to accomplish that?

_____

_____

_____

_____

13. In what areas does our society or culture encourage us to ignore self-control?

_____

_____

_____

_____

14. How does self-control change as a person ages?

_____

_____

_____

_____

15. Are you able to exercise self-control more successfully as you age?

_____

_____

_____

_____

God's Promise

Hebrews 4:14 says that Jesus Christ not only knows but has also experienced our weaknesses: "For we do not have a high priest who is unable to sympathize with our weaknesses, but one who in every respect has been tempted as we are, yet without sin." God knows the areas with which we each struggle. He knows where we are weak. He will give us what we need to practice self-control. He will not leave us when we fail, but for the sake of His Son, He will forgive our sin and strengthen our self-control. Trust in Him to guide you as you practice self-control.

Challenge of the Week: Focus on an area in which you struggle with self-control. Ask for God's help as you strive to live a life pleasing to Him.

Closing Prayer: Dear Father in heaven, we come to You as people who have a hard time practicing self-control. We always want just what we want, and we often behave in ways that are very selfish. Walk with us this day and every day, giving us strength to practice self-control so that we may live according to Your will. In Your Son's name we pray. Amen.

LEADER'S GUIDE

Week 1: The Love of Ruth

1. We are to show love for others because hatred is destructive to ourselves and to others. God Himself seeks vengeance.

2. Answers will vary.

3. It is not our love alone that covers sins, it is by the love of Christ Jesus that sins are forgiven. Christ covers all sins by His blood poured out for us on the cross.

4. This verse tells us that we are to show to all people the kind of expansive, generous love that we show our own family members. After all, in Baptism, we are made to be brothers and sisters!

5. Christ's love for the church was sacrificial and complete. He gave Himself fully for His Church. Husbands and wives are to follow His example of selflessness.

6. Answers will vary.

7. Ruth is set in Moab, a foreign land for her. There has been a drought and a famine, increasing the hardship that widows must endure.

8. In this historical time period, women without husbands or sons had no secure means of support. She probably felt very alone and destitute.

9. They loved and respected her so much that they wanted to stay with her. Even though Naomi told both of the women to return to their own homes, Ruth asked to stay with Naomi because she was so devoted to her.

10. Ruth pledges her commitment from this moment until her death to Naomi and to her "people," who are the children of Israel. This exhibits familial love, but more than that, it shows the depth of her love for the Lord.

11. Answers will vary, but should include that God has commanded us to love one another. The love for family can bring many blessings.

12–17. Answers will vary.

Week 2: The Joy of Elizabeth

1. The psalm writer's joy—and ours—are found in the Lord God.

2. Joy, and with it relief, come in the morning.

3. Praising God is a response that comes from our love for Him. It is appropriate, expected, and continuous.

4. This verse refers specifically to the altar in church.

5. Joy that comes from salvation in Christ is undeniable and lasting. Therefore, no one can take it from us.

6. This side of Christ's return, we will experience troubles of various kinds. But we are not defeated by such troubles because we have Christ's promise of mercy and salvation.

7. Joy and gladness.

8. Her baby leapt in her womb and she blessed Mary and her unborn child.

9. Elizabeth had a strong faith in God and she knew that both she and Mary were blessed by God.

10. Scripture tells us she shared her blessing with those around her.

11. The Holy Spirit fills us with the joy of the Lord and we should share that joy with others.

12–17. Answers will vary.

Week 3: The Peace of Hannah

1. Obedience to God's Law brings peace because we are confident in Him.

2. Disobedience brings punishment. Obedience, therefore, brings with it abundant blessings.

3. This passage is a warning to us to heed God's commands. Doing so brings us peace in that we can be sure of His perfect plan of salvation for us.

4. In Christ alone.

5. This is an overall sense of peacefulness and well-being that comes when we are confident in the righteousness that comes only from Christ.

6. In our hearts. Answers to part two of this question will vary.

7. It is only by faith in God and unity with Him through Christ that we have peace in our hearts. This blessing is for us and for others.

8. Elkanah has two wives, Hannah, who is barren, and Peninnah, who has many children.

9. Even though Elkanah loves Hannah, she is very depressed over the fact that she is childless. During that time period, women who were barren were frowned upon.

10. While praying, she surrendered all to God.

11. Answers will vary, but should include that as Christian women, we are to surrender all to God.

12–17. Answers will vary.

Week 4: The Patience of Mary, Mother of Jesus

1. Answers will vary.

2. Yes, certainly.

3. To show patience first and foremost.

4. By the Holy Spirit, we have faith in Christ's resurrection and ours. Our patience, then is strengthened by the assurance of Christ's love for us.

5. We are to endure obediently, and we do that by the strength that is renewed as we receive the gifts of the Lord's Supper.

6. Our compassionate and loving heavenly Father shows us, His beloved children, undeserved and vast patience.

7. Mary was probably both frightened and awestruck.

8. Because she was pregnant, it was probably a very uncomfortable trip for her.

9. Mary experienced a typical mother's first reaction . . . fear.

10. Most mothers would typically feel upset by being slighted by their own child.

11. Answers will vary, but should include that by trusting in God, we can learn to patient in all things.

12–17. Answers will vary.

Week 5: The Kindness of Abigail

1. Answers will vary.

2. Because we do not intentionally cause harm to ourselves, the Lord expects us to treat others with the same compassion, understanding, patience, and kindness that we show to ourselves.

3. We are to show kindness, compassion, tenderness, and mercy to others.

4. We are!

5. Our heavenly Father, shows us undeserved and unrestrained love and mercy. Because He is God, He can do nothing else.

6. We can depend on God to show us compassion and mercy, to be faithful to us.

7. The Bible tells us that he was harsh and evil.

8. Abigail is described as good, understanding and beautiful.

9. David and his men were afraid to approach Nabal due to his reputation, but they did so out of a sense of justice.

10. Abigail was a compassionate woman, caring for others even when her husband would not.

11. Answers may vary, but should include that God expects us to treat others with the love of Christ.

12–17. Answers will vary.

Week 6: The Goodness of Dorcas (Tabitha)

1. Goodness.

2. We will have life with God.

3. Jesus is stating that He is God the Son.

4. God pleasing behaviors, such as goodness, are learned behaviors. They do not come naturally to us.

5. We are created for a God-given purpose. Our good works are a response to God's gift of salvation through Christ. God created these works for us to do as part of His plan for us.

6. Dorcas is described as a disciple.

7. Dorcas is known for her love of God, her kindness, goodness and compassion.

8. Many people implored him to come.

9. By that of the Lord. Peter knew that many would be brought to the Lord by this event.

10. She was able to bring others to God by being a role model and through the miracle of being brought back to life.

11–16. Answers will vary.

Week 7: The Faithfulness of Deborah

1. We are assured of God's rock-solid faithfulness.

2. God's faithfulness is boundless; it extends farther than we can imagine.

3. Regardless what happens to us, God provides us the only means of escape from our sin—Jesus Christ. We can endure whatever befalls us because we have confidence, a gift of the Holy Spirit, in God's enduring faithfulness to us.

4. Through Christ's sacrificial death on the cross for us, God forgives us. He can do nothing else because He is God.

5. Through the washing and regeneration of the waters of Baptism, God's mercies to us are continual.

6. We are bound by the prison of our sinful nature and by the devil. But as baptized and redeemed children of God, we have the gift of faith, which will never be taken from us. By relying on the Lord's strength and mercy, we can endure all that this life throws at us.

7. Women were typically not in positions of power. God, in His infinite wisdom, knew that only Deborah could carry out His will.

8. As a prophetess, Deborah was inspired by God to deliver a message.

9. She faithfully responded to God's call by completing the tasks she was given: settling disputes and guiding Barak.

10. Barak and the Children of Israel benefited by being victorious war and living in peace for 40 years afterward.

11. Answers will vary but should include that God can use anyone and any circumstance to carry out His will.

12–17. Answers will vary.

Week 8: The Gentleness of Mary, Sister of Martha

1. Because the Lord is with us, His baptized and redeemed children, and has shown us boundless mercy and forgiven all our sins. Therefore, we are able to extend to others the same kind of gentleness and kindness that we have already experienced.

2. God-pleasing behaviors.

3. God, in Christ Jesus, does the heavy lifting for us. We no longer bear the burden of our sin. He took that upon Himself and bore the punishment on our behalf.

4. It is human nature to be proud. Gentleness and humbleness come only when we acknowledge what Christ has willingly done for us.

5. We are to show others the same mercy, forgiveness, patience, and love that Christ first showed to us.

6. One setting is a dinner at the home of Martha and Mary and the other is a dinner in Jesus' honor at another home.

7. Mary, unlike her sister, Martha, had her priorities straight. She knew the importance of being in the presence of the Lord.

8. Martha was too busy with earthly things to sit at the feet of Jesus, while Mary understood that the time with Jesus was short and she wanted to honor Him while in His presence.

9. Mary knew the Jesus was Lord and wanted to show Him honor and respect.

10. By defending Mary's actions with kind words, Jesus did indeed treat her with gentleness and kindness.

11–16. Answers will vary.

Week 9: The Self-Control of Esther

1. We are out of control and without guidelines or order of any sort.

2. These are admirable qualities and God-pleasing behaviors for all people.

3. Answers may vary but should include virtue, knowledge, self-control, steadfastness, godliness, affection, and love. Note that each of these behaviors builds on the one that precedes it.

4. By seeking first God's will for our lives, we make deliberate choices about living in this world and not conforming to it. We are encouraged to do this and strengthened for it by regular worship, daily Bible study, and prayer. These behaviors are, however, responses to the salvation that Christ has worked for us. It is God who changes us in the water and the word of Baptism.

5. Esther, a Jewish girl, has been chosen as a wife of Ahasuerus, king of Persia.

6. She planned meals for the king, gaining his trust.

7. She was able to save the Jewish people from slaughter.

8. The original order to kill the Jewish people might have been carried out.

9. God is omnipresent, so of course He was with Esther and her people. That His name is not mentioned should not detract from the fact of His constant presence and power in the lives of those who love Him and for their benefit.

10. Esther's self-control is a result of her deeply held faith in God's power and provision for His people.

11–16. Answers will vary.

GOLDEN FRUIT

living the fruit of the Spirit
through the best times of your lif

> The fruit of the Spirit is love, joy, peace, patience,
> kindness, goodness, faithfulness, gentleness,
> self-control; against such things there is no law.
>
> Galatians 5:22–23 ESV

We are called to be daughters and wives, sisters and friends, mothers and grandmas. We are called to be volunteers, employees, citizens, and leaders. And as we fill these various roles, we are to be intuitive, creative, persistent, supportive, and productive.

Is it any wonder that we may also be tired and crabby?

This nine-session Bible study helps the Christian woman put all of these roles, characteristics, and emotions into perspective. Each session focuses on one fruit of the Spirit and considers how the lives and stories of nine biblical women convey that characteristic. As you study women like Esther (self-control) and Dorcas (goodness), Ruth (love) and Elizabeth (joy), you'll see how God is at work in your life too and how His promise of salvation and peace through Jesus are fully yours all the time.

For individuals and small groups, this Bible study includes questions that dig deep into Scripture and make personal applications of Jesus' Gospel to your life.

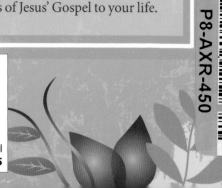

P8-AXR-450

Concordia
Publishing House
www.cph.org

ISBN 13   978-0-7586-3441-2
ISBN 10   0-7586-3441-2

9 780758 634412

Bible Study / Topical
20-3995